ABC SCIENCE RIDDLES

by Barbara Saffer

illustrated by Jennifer Johnson Haywood

An ABC Riddles book from Peel

63	
Eu	
151.965	

Text copyright©2001 Barbara Saffer
Illustrations & design
copyright©2001 Jennifer Johnson Haywood

Published by Peel Productions, Inc.
PO Box 546
Columbus NC 28722

http://peelbooks.com

Printed in Hong Kong

L_____y of Congress Cataloging-in-Publication Data
Saffer, Barbara.
    ABC science riddles / by Barbara Saffer; illustrated by
Jennifer Johnson Haywood.
        p. cm.
"An ABC riddles book."
ISBN 0-939217-55-4 (alk. paper)
1. Science--Miscellanea--Juvenile literature. 2. Riddles,
Juvenile. [1. Science--Miscellanea. 2. Riddles. 3. Alphabet.]
I. Haywood, Jennifer Johnson, ill. II. Title.

Q163 .S15 2001
500--dc21   00-068107

For Chelsea Troy and Brandon Kyle,
who like riddles.   –BS

For my eight grandparents—I am
lucky to have you.   –JJH

a _ _ _ _ _

My name starts with letter A.
I have a pleasant smell.
I'm sometimes used for trinkets
that artists make and sell.
During prehistoric times,
I oozed from trunks of trees,
lots of things got trapped in me—
like spiders, ants, and bees.
People travel far and wide
to look for chunks of me.
I'm a light brown resin.
Can you guess what I might be?

b _ _ _ _ _ _ _

I'm a tiny living thing.
My name starts with a B.
I'm found everywhere on Earth—
in air, the soil, and sea.
I make dead things decompose
and spoil old milk and cheese.
I also cause infections
and lots of dread disease.
I can form balls or rods,
or spiral like a curl.
Can you say my name out loud?
Go on. Give it a whirl!

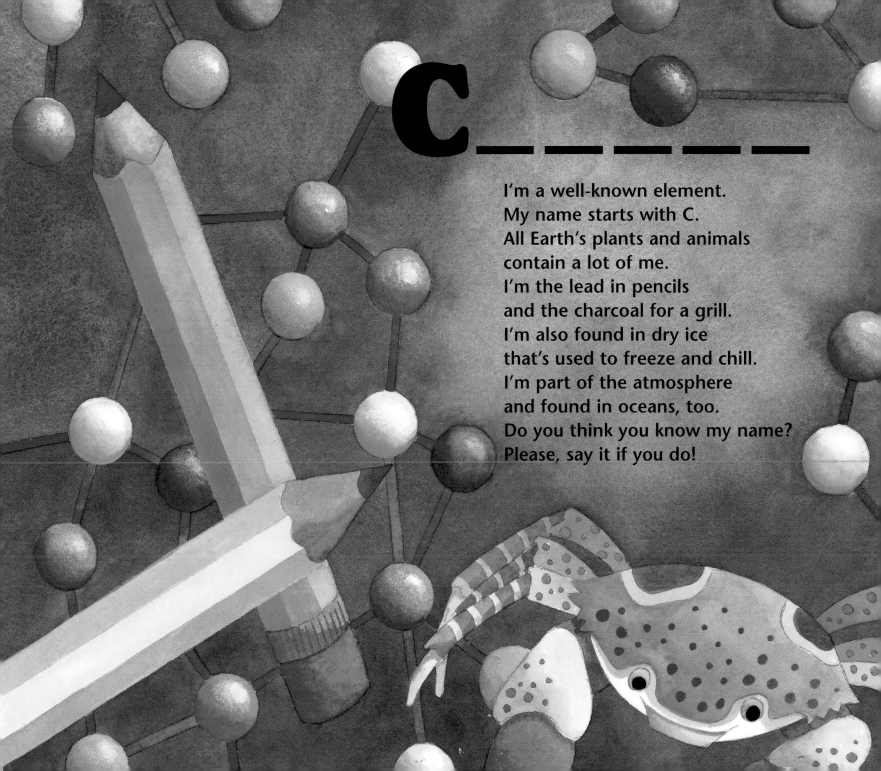

C_____

I'm a well-known element.
My name starts with C.
All Earth's plants and animals
contain a lot of me.
I'm the lead in pencils
and the charcoal for a grill.
I'm also found in dry ice
that's used to freeze and chill.
I'm part of the atmosphere
and found in oceans, too.
Do you think you know my name?
Please, say it if you do!

d_ _ _ _ _ _ _

My name starts and ends with D.
I form in deep hot stone.
I'm a tough hard substance
that can cut through steel and bone.
Sometimes, I am a lovely gem
that's colored blue or white.
I'm made of carbon atoms
that glitter in the light.
Mines in southern Africa
have many chunks of me.
Do you think you know my name?
Please, say it and we'll see!

e_____

I begin with letter E.
I happen way up high,
when the moon blocks out the sun
and darkens the whole sky.
I'm not seen too often—
only once or twice a year.
Please, don't ever look at me
without the proper gear.
Scientists may travel far
to see me really well.
Do you know what I am called?
This is the time to tell!

f＿＿＿＿＿

I start with F and I've been left
by life of long ago.
I might be shells, or teeth, or bones,
or mammoths trapped in snow.
I'm all that's left of dinosaurs,
ground sloths, and dodos, too.
And I could be a cave man's skull
or old preserved bamboo.
I'm sometimes found in rocky cliffs
or ancient tarry pits.
Do you think you know my name?
Go on now. Use your wits!

g— — — — — —

My name starts with letter G.
I'm scalding hot and wet.
I can rise a few feet high
or soar up like a jet.
I start as deep warm water
with hot rock at my base.
And when I heat to boiling,
I shoot out of that place.
I'm found in many countries
and parks like Yellowstone.
Do you know the name for me?
Call out in a loud tone!

h _ _ _ _ _ _

My name starts with letter H.
I'm common in all stars.
I'm also found on planets—
like Jupiter and Mars.
I am a gaseous element
that's light and has no smell.
I can make balloons float high,
above a steeple bell.
A scientist named Janssen
first found me long ago.
Folks call me a noble gas.
What am I? Do you know?

i__

I start with I and can be found,
in places that are cold.
Folks with skates can skim on me
or leap high, if they're bold.
I melt to form big puddles
or even smoky steam.
I'm used to make a tasty treat
that is a kind of "cream."
Penguins in Antarctica
may build twig nests on me.
Search your mind. What is my name?
Now, shout it out with glee!

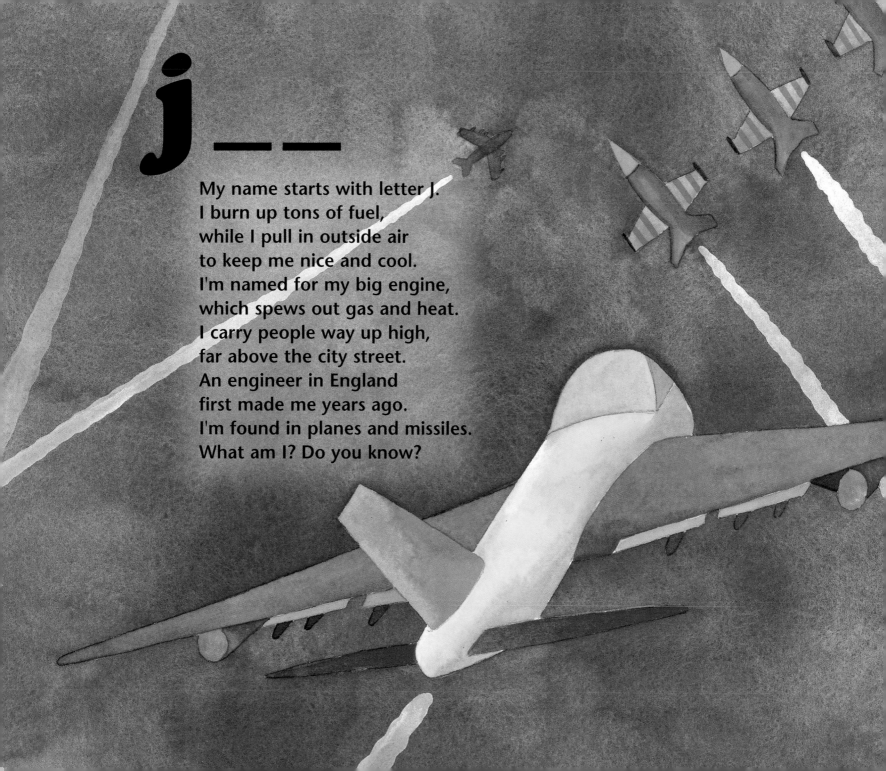

j __ __

My name starts with letter J.
I burn up tons of fuel,
while I pull in outside air
to keep me nice and cool.
I'm named for my big engine,
which spews out gas and heat.
I carry people way up high,
far above the city street.
An engineer in England
first made me years ago.
I'm found in planes and missiles.
What am I? Do you know?

k _ _ _ _

I'm found in deep blue oceans.
My short name starts with K.
My base is moored to big rocks,
so I don't drift away.
I have a stalk and brown blades
that some folks like to eat.
I'm seaweed used for sushi,
a tasty Asian treat.
I'm used to make some products—
like food that helps plants grow.
Can you guess what I might be?
Please, tell me if you know!

1___

My name starts with letter L.
I'm wet and scorching hot.
I flow out of cracks in Earth,
as dust blasts like a shot.
I may build thick sheets of rock
or large volcanic cones.
Both Iceland and Hawaii
are made of my dark stones.
In the western USA,
I form a broad plateau.
I'm also seen on Venus.
What am I? Do you know?

m _ _ _ _ _ _ _ _

The letter M begins my name.
From outer space I hail.
I cross the sky with streams of light,
as down to earth I sail.
I smack down with a ping or crash,
depending on my size.
And, if I'm really big and fast,
a crater can arise.
Then, dust may fill the atmosphere
and sunlight may not glow.
I killed off lots of dinosaurs.
What am I? Do you know?

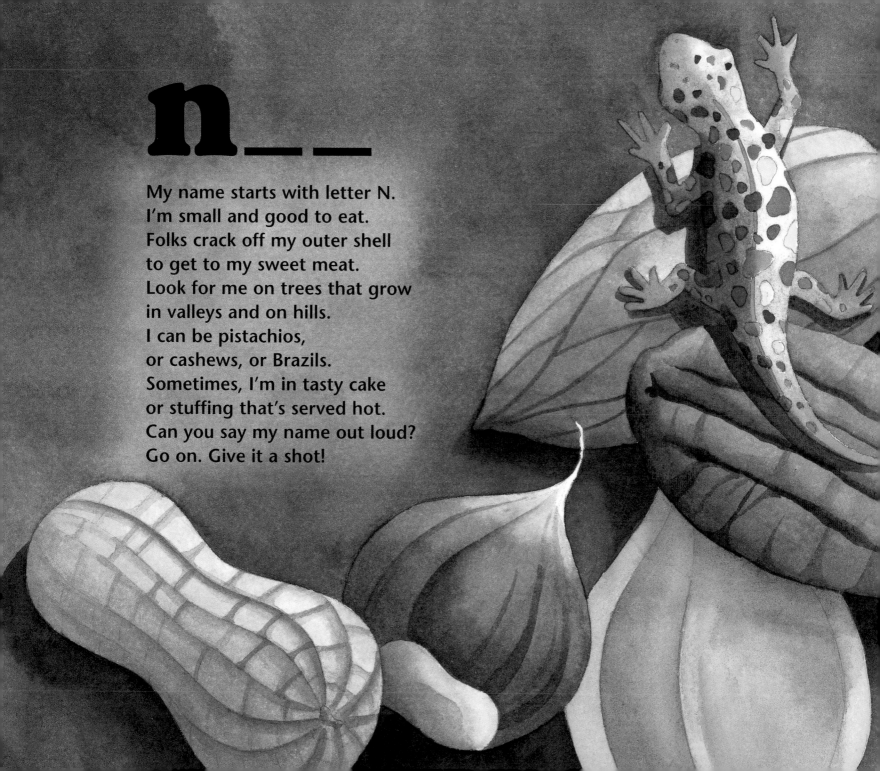

n＿＿

My name starts with letter N.
I'm small and good to eat.
Folks crack off my outer shell
to get to my sweet meat.
Look for me on trees that grow
in valleys and on hills.
I can be pistachios,
or cashews, or Brazils.
Sometimes, I'm in tasty cake
or stuffing that's served hot.
Can you say my name out loud?
Go on. Give it a shot!

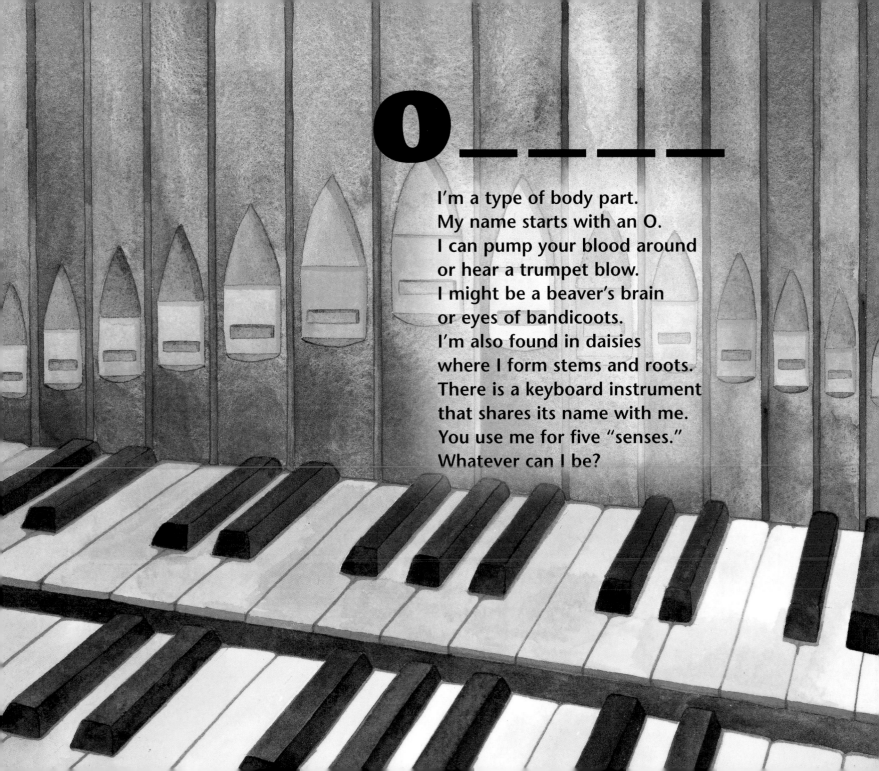

O _ _ _ _

I'm a type of body part.
My name starts with an O.
I can pump your blood around
or hear a trumpet blow.
I might be a beaver's brain
or eyes of bandicoots.
I'm also found in daisies
where I form stems and roots.
There is a keyboard instrument
that shares its name with me.
You use me for five "senses."
Whatever can I be?

p_____

I start with P and may contain
tons of gas and dust.
Sometimes, I'm a rocky sphere
with oceans and a crust.
Nine of me fly round the Sun;
one of my kind is Mars.
I'm also found in distant space
circling other stars.
One globe like me has humans;
it's colored green and blue.
Do you think you know my name?
Call out now, if you do!

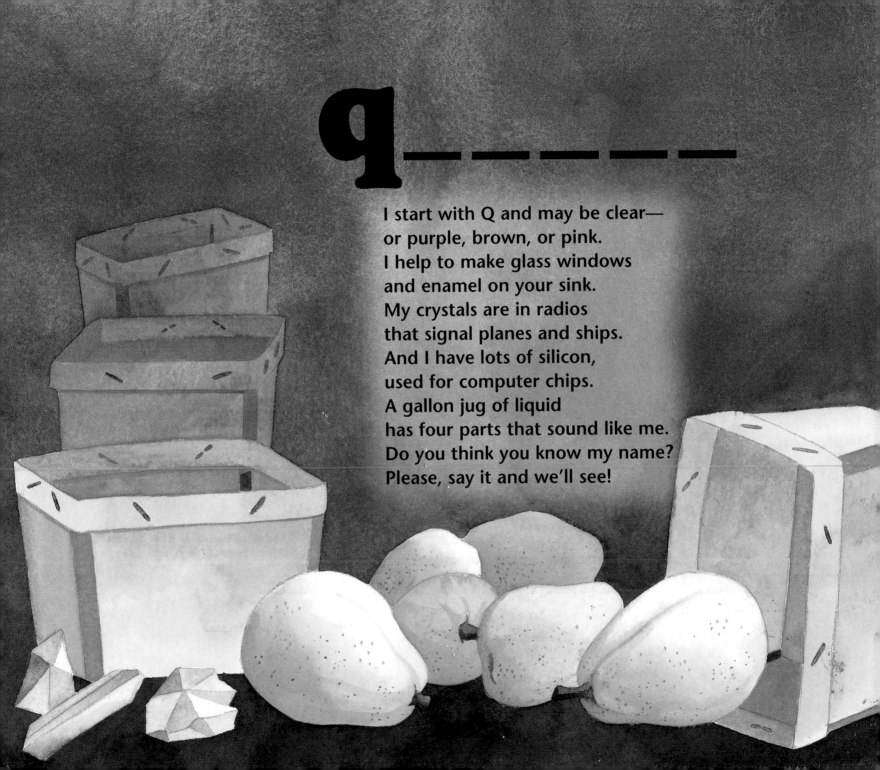

q_ _ _ _ _ _

I start with Q and may be clear—
or purple, brown, or pink.
I help to make glass windows
and enamel on your sink.
My crystals are in radios
that signal planes and ships.
And I have lots of silicon,
used for computer chips.
A gallon jug of liquid
has four parts that sound like me.
Do you think you know my name?
Please, say it and we'll see!

r_ _ _

My name begins with letter R.
You'll find me in the sea.
My neighbors are bright fish and shrimp,
and crabs hide out in me.
I'm made of massive coral rock
by polyps, clams, and more.
Scuba divers come my way,
when they swim out from shore.
Near Queensland in Australia,
I run through the Coral Sea.
Out there I'm called "Great Barrier."
What is your name for me?

S_ _ _ _ _ _ _ _ _ _ _ _

I start with S and orbit Earth,
way up high in space.
Sometimes, I take photographs
and send them to home base.
I can track big hurricanes,
and transmit TV shows,
or watch a foreign army—
to spy on where it goes.
One of my kind is Landsat,
launched by the USA.
Some of my kind are space probes.
What am I? Can you say?

t_ _ _ _ _ _ _

I start with T and hang down from
a cloud that's thick and dark.
When I get large and touch the ground,
I'll wreck a house or park.
My whirling winds are very strong;
I'll lift a great big load.
I'm sometimes called a cyclone;
inside me, things explode.
Large weather stations track my path
and show me on TV.
In oceans, I'm a waterspout.
What name would you call me?

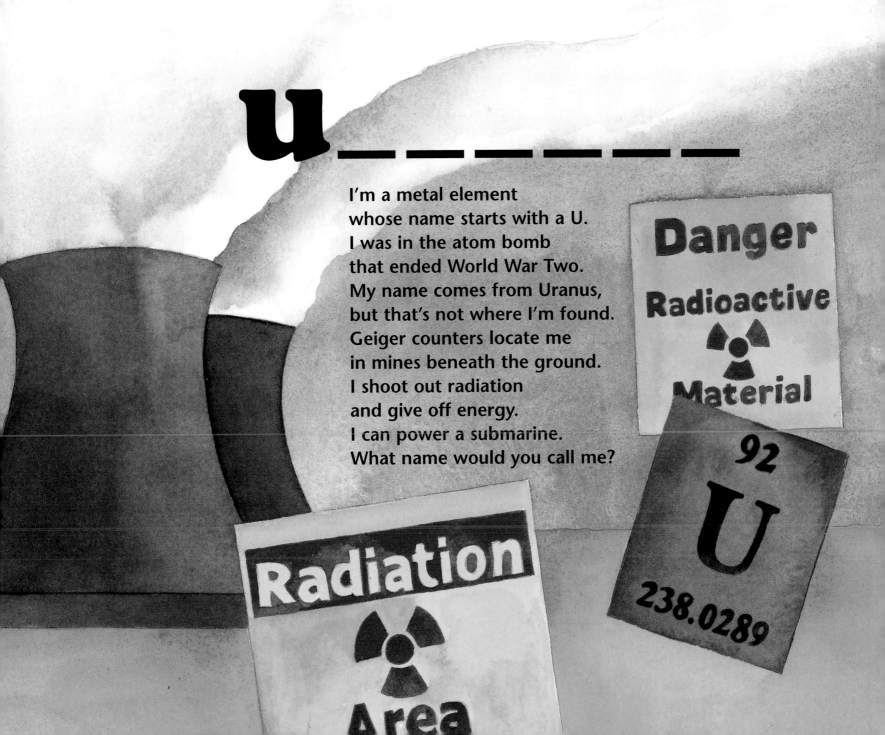

u_____

I'm a metal element
whose name starts with a U.
I was in the atom bomb
that ended World War Two.
My name comes from Uranus,
but that's not where I'm found.
Geiger counters locate me
in mines beneath the ground.
I shoot out radiation
and give off energy.
I can power a submarine.
What name would you call me?

Danger
Radioactive
Material

92
U
238.0289

Radiation
Area

V _ _ _ _ _

My name starts with letter V.
I'm moist and fill the air.
I can make a cloud that rains
on London or Times Square.
I'm the mist above a bath
and scalding smoky steam.
I'm water that evaporates
from a lake or stream.
I can form thick soupy fog
that makes it hard to see.
I'm a common gas on planet Earth.
What is your name for me?

W _ _ _

My name starts with W.
I sweep in from the sea.
Yacht and sailboat skippers
must keep an eye on me.
I spring up in the ocean,
when lively breezes blow.
I start out as a ripple
and swell up as I flow.
I roll past crabs and seastars,
as surfers ride on me.
I often crash on sandy dunes.
Whatever can I be?

_ _ _ _ _ X _

My name contains a letter X.
I'm found in outer space.
I race through the cosmos
at a very rapid pace.
My form can be a spiral
or oval like a grape.
And, sometimes, I'm uneven—
without a special shape.
I contain a lot of stars
plus gas in a huge cloud.
Think about the Milky Way.
Can you name me out loud?

y_ _ _ _

My name starts with letter Y.
Eggs have a shape like mine.
I can turn corn into beer
and change grapes into wine.
Though I'm a one-celled fungus,
folks buy me in a store.
I make sticky bread dough rise—
for bagels, buns, and more.
I can make B vitamins
that help you live and grow.
I'm also food for livestock.
What am I? Do you know?

Z _ _ _ _ _ _ _

My name starts with letter Z.
Kids study me in school,
when they need to know about
a bluebird, snake, or mule.
I tell folks that seals eat fish
and lions bite and maul.
I'm a branch of science
about creatures large and small.
Books about biology
describe me very well.
Many kids like me a lot.
What am I? Can you tell?

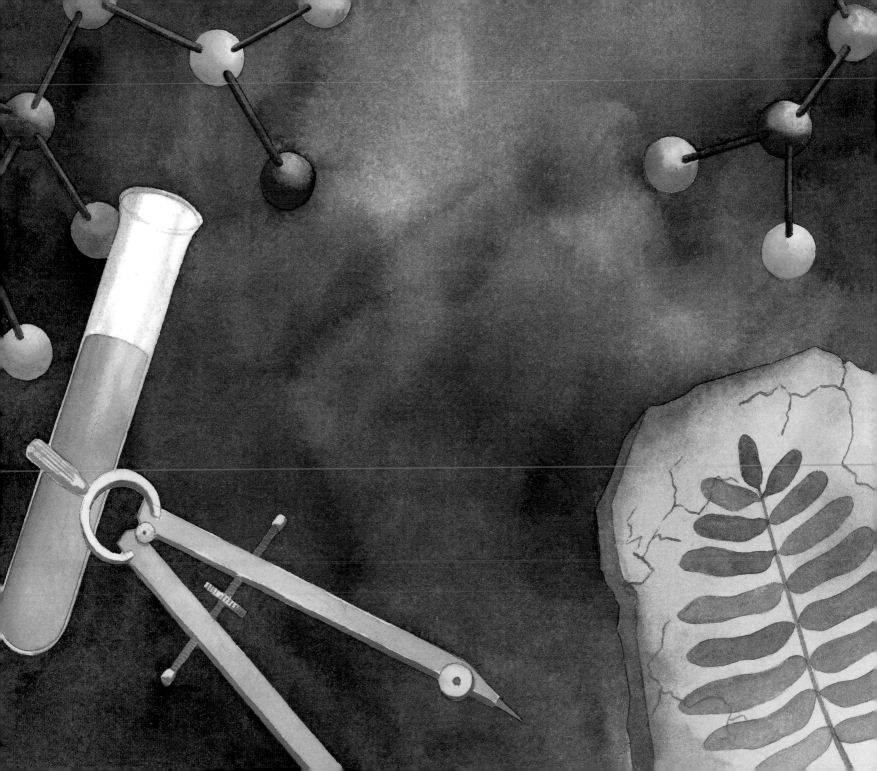

amber	jet	satellite
bacteria	kelp	tornado
carbon	lava	uranium
diamond	meteorite	vapor
eclipse	nut	wave
fossil	organ	galaxy
geyser	planet	yeast
helium	quartz	zoology
ice	reef	

Ideas for Parents and Teachers

Creating riddles that rhyme is a wonderful way to explore words. As you engage children in this poetic process, you will see them blossom in their vocabulary and their word comprehension. You will help them develop reading, writing, thinking, and vocal resentation skills.

Now encourage children to create more science riddles. Let them choose objects or processes they are curious about. Begin with letter and word clues.

- Start with a simple riddle such as this one for thunder:

    I'm seven letters long and I start with a T.
    When I roar and rumble, I'm loud as I can be.

- Stretch the exercise. Look up definitions in the dictionary. Find pictures of the subject. Add more rhyming lines with more clues to the riddle. End each riddle with a question, inviting others to answer the riddle.

- Share riddles! Most written riddles can be solved independently, but it's always more fun to try them out on other people. So, write down the riddles, perform the riddles, and see if others can figure them out.

- Instruct children to wait until all clues have been given before guessing the riddle. Have the child who guesses the answer first say the correct word, spell it out, then make up a new school riddle.

- As extended activities, encourage children to draw or sculpt the subjects of their riddles. Some may want to set their riddle to music.

Other children may want to create a series of riddles whose answers are clues to an even bigger mystery. For example, what do the answers to these riddles have in common?

The fun is limited only by you and your children's imaginations. Have fun with them!

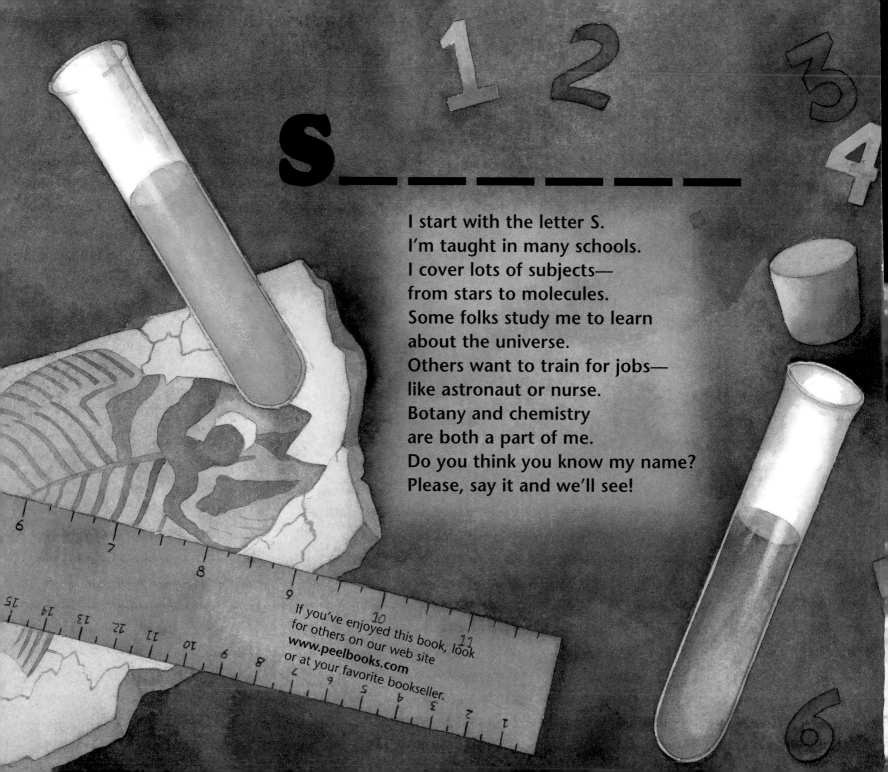

S_ _ _ _ _ _

I start with the letter S.
I'm taught in many schools.
I cover lots of subjects—
from stars to molecules.
Some folks study me to learn
about the universe.
Others want to train for jobs—
like astronaut or nurse.
Botany and chemistry
are both a part of me.
Do you think you know my name?
Please, say it and we'll see!